I0437994

Smacking the Muse

Thoughts, Stories, and Kung-Fu

by

Darin Waugh

Kiazen Publications

ISBN# 978-1-4357-3122-6

Acknowledgements

My children who make my heartbeat.
My martial arts mentors, training partners, and students, we
expect more of ourselves.
My family and friends for life's adventures and lessons.
God, who is life, the Muse.

Smacking the Muse

Introduction

If I go to bed in the evening and I haven't done any creative or reflective writing, I feel like the day is not complete. I'm sure many like me who love to write have the same prodigious desire to scribe. Even if I haven't worked on a book or an article, I may still log some scrap of  information that I heard on the radio, or document some clever quip a co-worker said, or moan about health problems—maybe vent about the state of politics or preserve some piece of philosophy or advice that came to mind. It's this deep-seated passion for reflection and writing that is the "muse." Trying to control this desire and discovering what to do with it is what I call *"smacking the muse."* If you have a yearning to create something, then you know what I'm talking about. You have to *smack* the impulse around to keep it focused, fun, productive, and positive; for the muse will always win one way or the other. What you reflective upon finds a way to invade your life. Join me as I square off with ingenuity and fight for control.

A special announcement. You!

A Bit of Me

My best friend, Tim Dukeman, introduced me to comic books in the fifth grade. We grew up in Columbus, Ohio during the 1970s. Tim and I enjoyed the comics so much we decided to create our own. So, we began to learn how to draw and create storyboards for our comics. Tim dedicated hour after hour on becoming a great artist and he succeeded. To this day, I still admire his dedication to everything he does in life. I tried to draw, but it just was not going to happen. Instead, I decided to write the stories for our comics and let Tim do the artwork. I found I enjoyed writing.

About this same time (mid 1970's), I discovered kung-fu movies and Bruce Lee. Bruce Lee became a big influence in my life and I began a lifelong study of martial arts (around twelve years of age). I found that Bruce Lee was much more than just a movie actor; a kung-fu master who created his own philosophy of martial arts called Jeet Kune Do (the way of the intercepting fist). Bruce was also a philosopher and writer. I wanted to be like Bruce. So, with my interest in writing and martial arts it only made sense that I would combine the two.

Now as a martial artist with over thirty years of experience, I want to share some of my journey with you. The life of a true martial artist is about finding honor through skill. This book honors life.

So perhaps "**Smacking the Muse**," is a style of mental kung-fu. Kung-fu means "to work." "Muse," means to reflect. Consequently then, I bring to these pages a certain contemplation—seeing life through the spirit of a modern American martial artist engaged in a creative battle.

Do not drive or operate heavy machinery under the influence
of a writer.

Smacking the Muse

Dojo

At the end of every class, we melted into a meditation pose with our legs folded underneath us in such a way that we sat on the tops of our feet. The small martial arts school didn't have air conditioning, so our workout created a pervasive heat. A heat so intense that condensation would cover the large mirrors at the front of the room. Still, we were to empty our minds, think of nothing, and settle our spirits. This is difficult enough to do under any circumstance but made nearly impossible when the textured design in the tile floor ate into the tops of our feet, and all the injuries from training—everything from pulled muscles to small bleeding cuts, are screaming at us. Much like life, when we seek peace, we are often met with discomfort. Staying calm and powerful in the face of conflict and pain is the martial artist's ultimate goal. Be a smart warrior!

Save a life enrich a soul.
And when the muse hurts.
Smack it!

Stare

Some beauty is delicate

        a peddle, a petite

Some beauty is hard

        a diamond, muscle

Beauty can be loud

        a tattoo, electric guitar

Often not the same meaning

        from your mind to mine

How women walk

Foreigners talk

Melodrama paints

        park our cars and wonder at it

            rain over the mountains

A good book and a better chair

Music changing spirits

Riding a classic motorcycle

Look, and look away

Before she catches me

Beauty needs a long stare

If your present situation is going well, you respect your past. If your present situation is difficult, you're likely to despise your past.

Stay in the present light. Even planning the future is posted in the "present." Treat the past as a lesson, not a hindrance.

Life is adjusting temperature!

The Stump

The student asked his Kung-fu teacher, "Master when are we going to remove that tree stump from our training yard, it's ugly and in the way?" The master nodded and rolled up his sleeves to get ready to train.

The next day when the student arrived, he looked at the stump and smiled. Perched on top of the stump sat a jade-colored vase of flowers. Beside the vase there was a silver statue of a dragon and beside the dragon sat a pitcher of drinking water.

The master entered the yard. "I thought you were going to get rid of that ugly stump?" the student asked.

"When you decorate the stump, you regain all possibilities."

The next day when the Master entered the training area, he saw the vase, the statue, and the pitcher sitting on a bench near the stump. On top of the stump, the student diligently worked on his kung-fu stances and techniques trying to stay balanced and fluid on the uneven stump.

"Ah, you thought the stump was in the way, but what have you discovered?" the Master inquired holding back a smile.

"I have discovered that even a stump can become part of the way."

Without hope destiny is failure.

Seek a great mentor and stay aware of the path that your search takes you on; for the path to the mentor also holds knowledge of the skills that you are trying to achieve.

Real intellectual advancement comes from debate. But you cannot debate the muse. It will never lose!

Create

Some are moved to understand and explain what is here, others want to create it.

So, the cycle goes, that some seek to study and understand what the creator has made (as God has made the universe and everything in it), and some are infected by the muse to create earthly treasures (in many forms), then if you meet a certain level of success and exposure, the explainers will seek to understand you as a creator as well.

One ultimate creator
Many apprentices

As a martial artist.
I can defeat an attacker's body.
I can defeat an attacker's mind.
But I prefer to join his spirit in peace.
For the warrior's true strength is his humanity.

Jukebox

An old seedy nowhere bar called, *"The Vacant Spot,"* had a 1950's style jukebox, dusty in the corner. Frank, a truck driver whose wife left him after thirty years of marriage, is standing by the jukebox with a beer in one hand and a quarter in the other. He looked at the selection of songs and said out load, though everyone else was sitting at the bar about twenty feet away, "Do you have any *my wife left me* songs?"

"No, sad music comes from these speakers," a calm male voice replied, as several red and blue lights flashed from inside the sides of the jukebox.

Frank looked around. "What the heck! Who is playing a trick on me? I've only had two beers."

"No tricks, just rhythms and rhymes to give the soul reprieve."

"So, the jukebox is talking to me—that's just great!" Frank stammered.

"It could be worse, I could be bouncing up and down on your toes," the jukebox replied. "You know you should have spent more time at home."

"Hey, that's personal, how do you know what's going on in my life?"

"Over the last forty years I've played every type of song. I know all the stories, all the emotions. Many songs come from years of personal struggle. You travel the road and leave your wife alone. When you're home it's difficult to keep contentment—dealing with all those things that should have been done already. Does that sound right?"

"Yea, but I have to make a living," Frank snapped.

"Yes, but perhaps you forgot to make a life?" The jukebox then played a verse from Sammy Kershaw's song *Haunted Heart*.

Go down the road called yesterday
Take a left on a lost highway
And make a right on memory lane

Drive until you feel the pain.

"I don't have to drive anywhere to feel the pain now," Frank moaned. "Every present moment is regret and I can't see my future road. I'm stuck at a dead end with my engine idling. I want her back, but I know life doesn't shift into reverse."

"Frank," the jukebox spoke in a loud voice this time, prompting most people in the bar to look at Frank, "You need a new song my friend, a new song!"

An unfamiliar tune with a modern country twang started to roar from the jukebox. Suddenly, everyone in the bar started to sing:

Figure out the reason and the range
Of what needs to be done to save your soul,
to make relationships whole
To bring love back into full vision
Takes a life changing decision

For,
when the road you travel
Separates you from love
Where are you really going
What are you going to accomplish

Need to,
make sure the route you take
Takes care of who you care for

Cause,
You know you're in trouble
When the jukebox talks to you

Love is the trip you're on

A journey calling you home

Cause,
What have you been through
When the jukebox talks to you

What are you going to do
When the jukebox talks to you

Dog Wisdom

I find it immensely interesting how Cesar Millan, the famous "Dog Whisperer," (who had a dog "rehabilitation" show on the *National Geographic Channel)*, often made great insights into human behavior, not just canine behavior. In the December 2006 issue of *National Geographic* magazine Cesar explained that "Dogs don't follow an emotional leader. They follow the dominant leader. We are the only species that follows an unstable leader." Perhaps this one reason why the state of the world is the way it is.

When asked, "What are the lessons we learn from dogs?" Cesar replied, "To live in the moment. Also, honesty, loyalty, integrity. Dogs will never stab you in the back or lie to you."

Writers accept a certain challenge in life, to see it, hear it, think it, experience it, and write it down so that it can be shared and preserved!

The muse dances, shift gears, it searches for the wind, and stacks bricks; a fashion without season, a motive for creation, swirling in a generous and foreboding heart.

Why Muse?

According to Greek mythology, Zeus and Mnemosyne had nine daughters called the Muses. This is the origin of the word muse. If one of the Muses loved a man than the man's worries would disappear. Out of this came the idea that another person could become an artist's inspiration, their muse. Usually, a muse was a woman. Every woman that Pablo Picasso loved became a subject in his paintings.

Insight and creative awakening can originate from the spiritual word (either as dark force or from a righteous deity), or from animals and nature, etc.

I have said that God is the ultimate muse. We may not know what inspired God to creation, but that force is in us. We don't have the power to create time and space, but we can become a muse to each other and express the brilliance of our human potential in all of its glorious varieties.

Those who truly know what they want to do in life and pursue it are blessed. To achieve one's ultimate dream is Godly. It is the muse working.

Those who fail to follow their muse, carry a dense load, a foggy dread, and endure a special suffering.

Don't give up on the muse, pursue it as a hunt for survival, smack it when its waves become turbulent and those around you try to kill it. Find a way to live the dream, sustain its humanity and your unique message. The muse *lived* is one of life's concluding joys.

"When you succumb to fear, you are under the illusion that you can predict the future."

Jen Sincero

Respect

Is often misdirected by our youth.

They scream, "You don't disrespect me!"

To their high school dropout boyfriend…

To their drug using parents…

To their gang member friends,

looking for respect in a world of deception

and false ambition.

They don't seek the respect of respected people.

A teacher, a preacher, an author,

any one of a thousand examples.

Instead, they seek respect from those whose lives are misdirected and in despair.

The desire to have a "place" is understandable.

But respect is only as good as the value you place on yourself and those whom you interact with.

Have self-respect first and seek respect from those who live in high regard.

Decide

Emotions send you signals
Not answers to problems
Feelings create information
But often don't represent good decisions
Step back from emotion
Separate from feelings
Understand the signals and information,
that emotions and feelings provide
Then gain strength from what you've learned about yourself.
Change your fears and apprehensions into a sense of accomplishment
Seek confirmation
Solid council
Pray
Then make your decision, based on the changes you've made within yourself
Advance

Unique

There are approximately 6,602,224,175 (July 2007 estimate) people in the world, just think, if you come up with a unique idea, it's one of a kind among this astounding number. That means that among all the billions of minds in this world, you thought of something that no one else has. This is an extremely significant act, no matter what form it takes, invention, art, science, etc. This is a simple fact that is often lost.

The Muse made you unique to do uncommon things!

Writing

If this is my savior
Then let it scribe
Jesus in my pocket
I carry the Lord proudly
He saved me in eternity
But I have to manager this earthly exchange.

"No one gets to heaven without a fight."
From the song "*Armor and Sword*," by the band **Rush.**

Impression

An observant mother and her teenage daughter are enjoying a nice day browsing the local art festival. There are many booths with all kinds of paintings, sculpture, and crafts. The mom and daughter came across a large painting that caught their eyes. On one side of the painting are waves of muted colors, and on the other side are swirls of bold colors. "The mom asked her daughter, "How does this painting make you feel?"

"I don't know...it's a fun painting, like a roller coaster." the girl answered.

"I see that," the mom replied, "but do you think that you chose how this painting made you feel, or did the artist choose your feeling for you?"

"Good point, Mom..."

"Influence surrounds us," Mom continued, "You have to control how it affects you and how it makes you feel. Don't lose yourself in confusing messages."

Muse
A concept not fully captured.
Because it always escapes.

Life is allergic to easy.
No ten simple steps to anything.
No easy diet plans.
No easy way to beat addictions.
Change is a constant engagement.
Requiring a valiant effort.
When something claims "simple" or "easy"
It is likely a simple way to make money.
(Though writing, publishing, and marketing a self-help book for
example, is not easy again making my point!)
Easy or simple ways to change are often misleading!
This is not to say that these resources don't offer good
information.
But, to get you to buy into their products, advertisers appeal to
your desire for quick change by tapping into the brain's lazy
nature.

Change happens whether you make it happen or not! Create the life you wish to manifest, and the muse will respond accordingly.

Life needs good pizza!

Old Friends

Call an old friend
Make her new again
She knows the smile in your soul
Magnifies your life's role

Find time for an old friend
Memories flake new again
Eras and arenas reappear
When a shared past is brought near

A great fiend
Important as life itself

Actor and author Alan Alda explained during a radio interview what he believes it means to have a life of meaning, he said, "A life of meaning is when one has a lasting sense of satisfaction."

I write down encouraging things I have heard to fight my own laziness and to remind myself again and again of the work involved in *"Smacking the Muse."*

9/11

When the planes pierced the building
Fire roared
A wave of heat covered us all
The country became
One pain
One rescue
One needing justice
The pile held more than bodies and debris
It held the forlorn heart of a mighty nation

Osama

You live as a dead soul
A waste of life energy
The de-evolution
A haunting pit of smoldering silt
Those you trick into evil
Lose their humanity
Their salvation
Any righteous purpose
Unjustified
You and they become not

(It's tragic that I even need to write something like this. Written before the death of Osama bin Laden.)

A time of terror
A beautiful world
God's design of the yin and yang
We play fools, heroes, and the complacent

Never miss a great opportunity to shut up!

You can't predict all the day's challenges.
Still, life requires planning.
But demands flexibility and adaptability.

Utterance

We could have been a song.
Too much went wrong
Long nights, too many fights

Could be, should be
Vacationing by the sea
Not pushing for personal victory

We could have been a song
Two hearts singing along
Instead, we question...break up suggestion
Ending it all

We could have a song
A life of melodies
A verse, of a curse, all but gone
Change needs to come now
Are we capable of knowing how

To beat despair
The rhythm needs to repair
Songs, change, they can rearrange
Let's rock the blues in our soul
We can be the song
Of the dreams we made strong

A delicate balance

Parents stumble
To know what to say
When to say it
Loving, but not too critical or judgmental
To let go, but still guide
To sometimes say nothing and
stand as pillars of support
Planting wisdom in little cards or on slips of paper
when tears roll
funny stories change the mood
Giving faith and encouragement
when ice cream covers their faces
Acknowledging how special they are
while waiting for the pizza to cool
Remembering that a parent's ultimate job
is to create inspired memories

Eulogy

Be the voice
For the one who has gone home
Help him say goodbye
Thank you, I'm sorry, I love you;
Those things he used to say, for all to hear one more time –
whether laugh or cringe
Catch his character—the positive side!
Be the lyrics for a life that once sang
Remind us what his life taught us
Encourage us to learn from the life whose memory is passed on
to us.

What is the most delicate part of the human body? Emotion!

Profoundly tired
Working for a barely stable life
As if everything sits on a wobbly fence
Ready to fall
So much to be thankful for
Living, working, worshipping in the United States of America
Still, I'm profoundly tired
American life is American bills
Lower middle class—blended profoundly tired and climbing a broken ladder
Having something in my wallet,
my ten-year old car breaks down
Catching up on medical bills,
a root canal needs done
Profoundly tired
Ceremoniously wired
Circumstances beat me, and I denied my own vocation for too long
Bad relationships wasted years of laughter
I worked overtime again today
Profoundly tired
But, I have a roof, I have a 401K
A wife and kids I adore
I still fight for my dreams and
I can survive profoundly tired in America

Church Signs

You've seen them, church signs, with their clever epigrams such as, *"Many people want to serve God but only as advisor."* Of course, now you can find these sayings not only on your neighborhood church signs, but on the internet as well.

Need a new life? God accepts trade-ins
http://net-burst.net/quips/punchy.htm

Wall

The old kung-fu Master brought two of his students who tend to be impulsive to an area in their village where an old building used to be. The building had long been torn down except for one two story side wall. The Master walked the students to one end of the wall. The students had no idea what the bearded Master had in mind for them. They had arrived at the school thinking they were going to have a typical martial arts class. One student spoke up, "Ok, Master please tell us what's going on?"

The Master rubbed his plump belly with one hand and held a small old leather ball in the other. "I'm going to give one of you the ball and then you are to throw the ball back and forth to each other and try to catch it. The only rules are, you have to throw the ball towards the left or right from where it landed, and you cannot tell each other where to stand or where the ball is going to go. You each have to catch the ball three times."

The two students smugly walked so that each one stood on either side of the wall and began throwing the ball over the top of the wall. At first the students thought the old man must be crazy, and that this "exercise" is taking away from their time working on martial arts techniques.

Soon the two learned that this assignment, which first appeared to be a like a kid's game, is not easy. Time after time the ball flew over the top of the wall, and they were unable to catch it. Trying to catch the ball was made even more difficult by the bricks and stones that were littered all over the ground that were once part of the building.

After an hour of tossing the ball, the students were moving slow and breathing hard. ."Master, how long do we have to keep going?"

"Yea," the other one said, wiping sweat from his forehead, "We get the lesson, not everything is as easy it first appears. Now can we stop?"

"No," the Master barked, "You can't stop until you both have caught the ball at least three times, and you still have not seen the lesson in this exercise. Follow the rules!"

Another hour passed, with the ball going over and over the wall, and though there were many close calls, they only managed two catches. Near exhaustion, one of the students finally yelled to the other student, "Hey wait a minute, knowing Master there must be something more to this?"

The other student responded while catching his breath, "Don't talk to me the Master said, we can't talk."

No," the first student said, "He said we can't tell each other where to go to catch the ball, he didn't say we couldn't talk."

The second student struggled to get up from his knees where he had been resting. "That's it!"

"What's it?" the first student wondered as he saw the second student come around the wall and walk towards him. "You can't come over here!"

"Throw the ball towards me just to the left or right of where it landed." The first student demanded.

His partner yelled back, "But you have to be on the other side of wall."

"Throw the ball," he demanded again in a loud stern voice.

The second student reluctantly threw the ball to the right of the other student, but not so far that he couldn't catch it—and catch it he did. Still looking perplexed as the ball returned to him near his left, the first student also caught the ball. They were surprised that the Master did not interrupt them as they completed all six required catches.

"Good," the Master said, "now come here." The students walked to the Master as he continued, "When I gave you the rules, I didn't say anything about having to throw the ball over the wall. You saw restrictions that were not there. You saw a wall and naturally took it as an obstacle. Then a long time passed before you discovered the options that were there to complete the task. You put the wall between you, and you could not succeed. Life is about rules and options. Do not let the 'wall' make you lazy, or on the other hand, make you work too hard. Face obstacles with logical thought. How can you be sure to succeed in catching the ball, or achieving anything in life unless you understand the rules and options? Then you must cooperate with each other in order to achieve. This is kung-fu."

World war became
Vietnam
The cold war became
The terror war
Thousands before these
Thousands yet to come
Human knowledge evolves
But human nature never does

War
How we gauge our national strength.
Charity, how we gauge our country's compassion.
What if we could switch this around?
Compassion needs to be taught just like making war is taught

Make sure every fight, whether verbal or physical has a
victory worth winning?

Sappy

I had a vision without conviction
Until you
stroked my eyes
I had a love without sentiment
Until
adoration stunned my heart
I had a life without bearing
Until you and I
Found admission

Politics = performance art.

Political campaigns have become entertainment companies. Politicians are actors. We now face the possibility that our leaders are chosen more on their ability to entertain us than on their leadership qualities.

"A politician thinks of the next election—a statesman of the next generation." *- James Freeman Clarke*

Be that man
Leading with compassion—hand
Righteousness—stand

Be that man
Old fashion strength
With modern style
Working hard
So that Love is taken care of
Faithful, respectful, mentoring
Where purpose and focus drives
A man to
Change the world by making his realm stronger

There really is no "best," only champions, who get moments of time being on top. Find what makes you a champion every day.

Approach life like a musical instrument
Learn to play it well.

The path to contentment is easily miss-stepped. One tiny wrong step can take you miles from the path.

Then-

Depression, when reality beats down your dreams Smack it!

Then-

Remember, the *Muse* will try to defeat you: to make you strong enough to handle the dream!

Then-

Commit with a strength that forces you to hit back and to outlast the desire.

"I like damaged people!"
Stephen Colbert

"Curiosity is the key to a great artist."
Ang Lee

"The legacy of our troops needs to be a better America."
Barack Obama

"Nothing stops a bullet like a job."
(Some guy on NPR, didn't catch his name, but this is an important statement!)

"Exposed ego is a weakness."
Jamie Fox

"The consistent, sustainable success that lets you live life on your own terms must be designed."
Mike Zimmerman

Muse calls
its victims to study, to originate,
to preserve; to stand in the rain and feel sunshine; to bear
inspiration like an infliction; vexed in the intrinsic magic of a
soul that must inspire.

Get me a guitar and I'll be OK!

Greetings

At work, I visit people in their homes, most are older retired people. Here are some of the clever greetings I hear from patients. I work for a home respiratory company.

Me, "How are you?"
Customer, "Oh, I'm partly cloudy today!"

Me, "How are you doing today?"
Customer, "I'm doing OK, but I'm trying to get over it." This particular gun-loving older gentleman also said, "I need a job that goes from noon to one o'clock and gives you an hour for lunch, because that's all I'm good for."

Me, "How are you?"
Customer, "Well, I lost my mind and don't see any reason to find it?"

Me, "How are you?"
Customer, "I'm too soon old, and to late smart!"

Me, "How are you?"
Customer, "I'm stiff!"

When I went into one lady's house, she explained the messy condition of her home by saying, "Please excuse my house; it looks like the Devil went to Sunday school!"

When people ask me, "How's it going?" I like to answer, "It's going right out my wallet!" Sometimes I will answer by saying, "Oh, you know how it is, take the good with the bad, and hope you have some money left over!"

Sue DaBaco

Sue DaBaco, and I both went to Streamwood High School, in Streamwood, Illinois. We played in a rock band named, "**Valin**;" (1978-80). Sue displayed amazing singing, guitar playing, and song writing abilities even then, and she has continued to play music her whole life.  Currently, she is a well-known and respected lady of Chicago Blues, playing with her band "*Sue DaBaco and Wise Fools*." I'm extremely proud of her accomplishments.

Information about *Sue and Wise Fools* can be found at http://www.wise-fools.com/index2.shtml. Their first album is available at www.cdbaby.com/suedabaco.

The following is the lyrics to one of the songs on Sue's album, called *"Scourge."*

SCOURGE

Your emotion is real,
the perception undone,
it is the heart of the matter,
what you have is now completely gone.

I can show you the answer,
but you won't listen to me
and your stubborn resilience,
will destroy humanity.

The face in the mirror,
the only thing you can control,
but you're so fucking mindless,
and so proud in that role.

If you think that you are free,
you'd better think again,
your incapacitation,
is the silence of the lambs.

Scourge

Go ahead pull the trigger,
it's what we are destined to do,
to breathe in all the toxins,
and to blow out all the fumes,

of hatred and of fear,
our existential importance,
we are the scourge, the rot, and the cancer,
Dying to rule the world.

Scourge

Sue and I still talk about getting back together to play music someday. Somehow, we'll make it happen. Maybe we'll write a song like this:

High school, we started to play
Going to be rock stars – had so much to say
Graduation and college lead us astray
Still wanting to make music again some day

He went on to be a kung-fu master
She became a guitar blaster

Years have shipped by
But we both can't deny
There's something special in our views
As we both still SMACK THE MUSE

I became a guitar blaster
He's a kung-fu master

Life challenges us through the fears
But I know there's one who always cheers...for me;
knowing, we'll stand on the stage again
The guitar blaster and the kung-fu master
Friendship like ours always wins

It's the artist's job to enjoy the labor—everyone else's joy to labor over the results.

Life
Playing out the yin and the yang that God has put into motion! Good work, good health, good life

Doubt leads to apprehension. Staying apprehensive for too long allows fear and anxiety to keep building. Taking action is the only way to fix anything.

Gun

Here's a quick story that I originally posted on the Jeet Kune Do Brotherhood web site. Jeet Kune Do, is the martial arts philosophy formulated by the late movie star and martial arts master Bruce Lee. The title of the post was, "Have you ever had a gun pulled on you?' Here's my response:

Right out of high school, I started college and began working at a 7-11 store. Most of the time I worked third shift and quickly realized that the "freaks" do come out at night. The company taught us to not stay behind the counter at night whenever possible, especially when there were not any customers in the store. Instead, we should be out among the shelves, so that if someone did want to rob the store, they would have to get you behind the counter first. One night, a short scum-bucket dude came in the store and walked to front counter. He looked nervous and started pacing around in front of the counter. As recommended, I had been restocking shelves, but as I came to end of the isle, the guy turned enough so that I could see a gun inside his coat. I was sure he wasn't a cop or something related. So, I just stopped in my tracks and started running my mouth with small talk. I don't even remember what I said. He never answered back and I kept talking until he took a pack of cigarettes off a display and put it on the counter. I remember thinking, 'Well if he's going to rob me, here goes.' As I walked behind the counter, sure enough, he put his hand in his coat—but at the same time another customer came into the store. The dude ended up leaving without buying the cigarettes. So, I didn't technically get the gun pulled on me, but almost. Running my mouth, may has saved my life?

We had one female employee who wasn't as lucky as I had been. She was kidnapped from the store, rapped, and left on a country road. Another employee was tired up in the bathroom while the store was robbed.

My dumb ass ended up working for 7-11 for 5 years, and as you can image, I have many more stories. Working at a convenience store is the only job I told my daughters I would not want them to do!

Here's another story from my 7-11 days:

Beer Runs

One of the 7-11 stores I worked at was located at the corners of Frebis and Champion Avenues in one of Columbus, Ohio's worst neighborhoods. A favorite activity of the delinquents who lived in the area involved coming into the store and grabbing twelve packs of beer out of the coolers and then running out of the store. Usually, this would involve four or five guys and between them all, they could run off with a whole party worth of beer. We called this type of theft a *beer-run*.

On most weekends we were allowed to have two people working third shift. Again, I was in my twenties, and I worked a lot of third shifts with a co-worker named Bill. Bill was also in his twenties.

After we experienced a number of these beer-runs, Bill decided we should do something about it. Of course, management did not want us to directly confront robbers. Bill came up with a plan anyway. He unscrewed the handle from one of the mops and laid it on the floor behind the counter in the cash register area. The register area was near the middle of the store, so the beer runners had to run past the register to leave the store.

The mop handle only laid on the floor for a couple of hours until we got a beer-run. Five dudes came in and each of them grabbed two twelve packs of Miller bottles and took off running for the door. While the guys were grabbing the beer, Bill positioned the mop handle on the floor to where he wanted it. Then as the first guy ran past the counter, he kicked the broom handle out from under the counter towards the thieves. I doubted that this trap would even do anything, but much to my surprise it worked. As the mop handle slid out from under the counter the beer-runner tripped over it, and he yelled as he fell on floor dropping his beer. Several of his buddies then went flying over top of him falling all over each other. Beer also went airborne, and we heard bottles breaking as they hit the floor. I became concerned that these guys might turn on us. Instead, most of them started laughing, probably because they were smoking something before they came into the store. Then they picked themselves up while grabbing what they could of the unbroken bottles and left the store.

Bill and I also laughed, as we spent the next half hour picking up broken glass and mopping up beer from the floor. I still worried about these guys coming back after Bill and me. They never did, and 7-11 eventually closed this store in that neighborhood.

Prankster

Here's another story I posted on a website. The site asked people to post their experiences of being in a real street fight. I've had my share of fights but decided to post a story about how I ended up dealing with a prankster.

This technically is not a fight story, but more of how I had to give a prankster a lesson in respect. This incident took place when I was in college and working part time at a discount store—so I was in my twenties. I also studied and taught martial arts. Anyway, some big lug nut guy that also worked at the discount store decided to make me a victim of his childish pranks. Why he chose me I have no idea, and he didn't have any idea that I studied martial arts.

This jerk would walk up behind me and flick the back of my ear or walk by where I was pricing merchandise and knock the price gun out of my hands. One time while eating soup in the lunchroom, he pushed my soup bowl to the other side of the table. He would throw packages of socks at me, etc. This is the kind of stupid and annoying crap that he would do. I kept asking him to stop and he might for a while, but then he just couldn't resist the temptation to do something else like mark up with a pen some paperwork I was working on.

This flunky had size, at least five inches taller than me and he outweighed me by a hundred pounds, but I could tell he was not very athletic. He annoyed me more than he threatened me. I knew my turn would come, especially since he ignored my requests to stop bothering me.

Finally, my chance to end his carnival came when we were pricing soft goods in the warehouse basement and no one else was around. There were boxes of product stacked around us taller than our heads. No noise but the click, click, click, of our price guns as we priced packages of dishrags and kitchen towels. When all of sudden I looked up to see man-brat swinging a four-foot dowel rod at me in a challenging and threatening way. I remember thinking, *if he gets within a foot of me, then that's it*, and woo…., the stick came close to my face—now we're at a whole new level. A level I felt comfortable at. I took the package of dishrags that I had in my hand and I threw it at him to distract him. As he tried to block the dishrags, I blasted a sidekick right into the middle of his chest. The stick flew out of his hand, and he slammed into the stack of boxes behind him and fell to his knees. As he got up trying to catch his breath, he had a completely startled look on his face. I had to keep from laughing because the white dress shirt he wore had a perfect footprint of my size tens on his chest. But I kept my composure and barked to him, "I could have kicked you in the throat you dumb fuck, don't mess me ever again!" He never bothered me anymore, matter of fact; he went to great lengths to avoid me. Lesson learned!

Spin Reality

A spinning mirror catches everything...briefly
But as the mirror turns it can miss so much
Stop the mirror and look forwards and backwards at the same
time
Thrive in these captured bits
Smile at yourself, look over your shoulder
The muse works in reflection
Spin your field of vision again

Those of us lost in possibilities and too many interests suffer in a relentless search for satisfaction. Smacking the Muse is essentially finding focus—the center of your creative desire. The multi-artist (a creative person who has many outlets), needs shaped into a limited scope, for once focus is imposed, then control and time management will lead to a successful creative process.

Convincing the nature of humans to turn from greed to righteousness is the most difficult thing there is.

Losing Generations

I used to work for a home respiratory company. I delivered oxygen equipment to every type of home imaginable. On one delivery I could be in a house crawling with roaches, and the next house could be a giant mansion covered in marble. I've delivered medical equipment to the famous, the homeless, and even to those incarcerated.

The one thing that bothered me the most was how many kids that I saw who suffered intellectual neglect. I've been to homes where young toddlers and kids are offered no intellectual stimulation; no toys, no crayons, no books, nothing! Most of the time these kids just sat on the coach or on a bed with nothing to do but to stare at the lazy adults who were not "raising" them. It's tragic!

I remember one time I left a house with kids in the above situation to find a group of people standing around a car that was parked in the street, eating fast food chicken dinners, when all of sudden they started throwing biscuits at each other. Then they just threw the chicken boxes in the street and drove off. When I got in my truck and pulled around the corner on my way to my next delivery, a bank on the corner was surrounded by the police. The bank had just been robbed.

The amount of drama that goes on in some of these neighborhoods is often amazing. We're losing generations of kids and productive neighborhoods for kids to grow up in. About 7,200 students a day drop out of school in this country, and I have no doubt that many of them come from homes where lazy parents offered no intellectual stimulation to their children.

I'm not talking about those who are poor. I could tell the difference between those who are poor and those who are lazy. The "lazy" by virtue of their lack of motivation to contribute to their families and society, end up "stealing" from their families and society. The poor do all they can to help their families, themselves, and society, they just may be lacking in resources, education, or have health problems, etc. Kids in poor homes still have emotional support and things to do, even if it's just reading books from the library.

The fact that we continue to lose so many kids into lives of intellectual laziness is a true American tragedy.

Urinal Religion

Often some well meaning Christian leaves a religious pamphlet on top of the urinals in men's rest rooms. Most of the time I ignore the pamphlets, and depending on my mood, I've even thrown them away—because as a Christian, this is embarrassing! Christians trying to save you even as you take a piss. It seems like a desperate way to spread the good news. But, who knows, maybe a soul or two has been saved at the urinal?

When I do pick up the pamphlet it usually conveys a desperately important message. The one I'm looking at right now is titled, *"Sincerely Wrong."* The pamphlet starts off with a story about an ambulance driver who after picking up an accident victim, drove into a flooded area and got the ambulance stuck. So, despite the ambulance driver's sincere desire to help the accident victim he ended up being "sincerely wrong."

Then the pamphlet poses the question, "Do you know if you're going to heaven?" Of course, it ties this in with the ambulance driver, making the point, that you may be "sincerely wrong" in your assumption as to whether or not you're going to heaven.

The pamphlet ends with several Bible passages that one should reference in order to know if heaven awaits.

Certainly, this urinal message is worth taking notice of. I just wish it hadn't been delivered by the Church of Zip and Flush!

Quips

Why is it that whenever someone says, "I'll keep this brief," he/she ends up talking forever?

She lost control of her sexy!

Who's sleeping in my pocket?

I wish my grandmother had lived long enough to see Press & Seal! She would have loved that stuff!

Safe for emotions is a mature love!

Two best words in the English language; open bar.

Three best words in the English language; you tested negative!

I need a new gravity to hold me up!

It's hard to play normal!

To love pizza is to love oneself!

Love is the granting of a partner exclusive permission to remind you of your flaws!

All the psychological trends and self-help mantras like "*The Secret*," or "*The Power of Positive Thinking*," work until your spouse or partner is mad at you. When your spouse or partner is angry at you, brilliant psychology breaks down!

You have to be a little strange to help the world to change.

Mantra: I am attractively flawed.

I am attracting serendipity.

Keep it interesting!

Dreams do have time limits!
There is a "too late" in "It's never too late."
Ambitions need good health and even more time.
Even the fiercely independent become dependent.
Hiding behind "never" are the scraps of lost opportunities.
Smack the muse before it slaps you out of the game.

"Whether you think you can or you can't, you're right!"
-- *Stewie from the TV show Family Guy*

Travelogues and Tales

In 1962 my Great Grandmother, Alice Grace Waugh, self-published a book of poems title, *Travelogues and Tales*. I wish I could have known her. Here is a poem from her book:

IN RETROSPECT

The light of the stars and the blue of the skies
Were mirrored in my Annie's eyes.
Of rouge or lipstick she had no need.
God was her artist and truth her creed.
And the hand that set the stars in the sky
Put the bloom on her check and the light in her eye.
My heart exulted with joy and pride
When Annie promised to be my bride.

"We'll journey together through life," she said,
On that wonderful morning when we were wed.
"By two our joys shall be multiplied,
Because we'll share them side by side;
And sorrows shall be cut in two;
You'll share with me and I with you."
Oh! Fair was the morning and fair was the bride,
When we stood at the altar side by side.

I built a house for my bride so fair;
A humble home; but love was there.
In a joyous circle three years went round;
And peace and love in that home were found.
God sent an angel our lives to bless
With a form of infant loveliness;
And, when that babe to our care was given,
This earth, to us, was a second Heaven.

For but a season God to us spared
The little darling whose love we shared.
It was hers and mine, yet God's as well;
And He took it home with Him to dwell.
We stood by the little grave, together,
Two anguished souls, in the Autumn weather;
And the clods that, down on that coffin fell,
Were dropped on our poor, bruised hearts as well.

The seasons come the seasons go,
With warmth and verdure or cold and snow.
In the endless circle of dawn to dawn,
One after another, the years have gone.
Time flung on my head his wintry snow;
And sad and lonely through life I go.
For now I journey bereft and lone;
And Annie's bed is a churchyard stone.

Temporary Headstone

My Grandmother's poem on the previous page, reminded me of a situation that one of my martial arts students experienced. I worked for the parks and recreation department in Columbus, Ohio while in college, and I taught an adult self-defense class. Linda, a single Mom with four school age kids living in a rough neighborhood joined my adult class.

Linda had a physically and emotionally abusive ex-husband who had moved out but would still show up at her house drunk and cause trouble for her and the kids. She wanted to take my self-defense class not only to defend herself but for exercise as well.

I could see her self-confidence build the more of my classes she attended, and we developed a friendship. She told me stories of the terrible situations that her ex-husband put her through.

Her stories were helpful and educational to me as a self-defense instructor and I'm sure I helped her by being there to listen.

One day Linda, who didn't have a car, asked if I would take her to a cemetery. I'm sure I looked a puzzled until she explained that it was the anniversary of her daughter's death.

In the car as we drove to the cemetery, she told me that her three-year-old had been playing in the yard and ran behind the car of a family member who was backing out of the driveway. The car ran over her and killed her. I could not have imaged the horror of that situation.

When we arrived at the cemetery, she led me to the spot where her daughter rested. There was not a real headstone, just a small 6"x6" temporary stone that the people at the graveyard furnished. Linda felt bad that even though her daughter had been dead for several years, she could not afford to buy a real headstone, and of course her ex was more interested in alcohol then he was in his family.

Linda and I placed a penny under the stone, and we sent out a prayer. Linda said the only thing she can do for her daughter now is to get her a real headstone.

After several months in my class Linda's ex showed up at the house drunk as usual, but this time she decided not to let him in. He forced himself in the front door and Linda felt justified in protecting her home. She punched him in the face which gave her enough time to grab a baseball bat. She used the baseball bat to beat him until he fell out the front door, and then she called the police. She said she would have never had the courage to do that without taking my class.

Eventually, Linda and I lost touch. I still think about that little grave marker and the tragedy of losing life's most precious gift.

Happiness is a battle.
Laugh at it daily.

Some

Some days thoughts worth writing come to you, the muse is strong and flowing.

Some days nothing comes to mind, and you need to revert to research before the feeling of not accomplishing anything ruins your day.

Some days you piggyback off something written by someone else and ride it into new twists and turns.

Some days you should just practice writing or creative exercises and wait for the muse to come out of hiding.

Some days you burn your pizza and should have it delivered and watch a good movie.

Museology, the study of the desire to be creative.

Martial Artist

Study with a forceful calm
Bowing to life with the fighter's spirit
And as you train
Expect to become a soul transformed by
a code infused through the old masters—transcribed by the
modern mind;
"Kiai," and step forward to a life of higher expectations

The muse is motion not just emotion.

Life is the ultimate lesson in the use of time.

My Kung-fu is better than your Kung-fu

Fuhua, a young man robust with the pride of just having defeated the best fighter in his kung-fu school, decided he needed to seek out a greater challenge.

He figured he could become a legend across China if he defeated the best fighter from the rival kung-fu school across town. His town of Hechi, is in the Yunnan-Guizhoe highlands.

The journey to the other school takes about an hour, so Fuhua put on his brightest blue training uniform, took a long drink of water and started to walk across town. As he walked, he noticed the common folds doing their routine jobs, washing laundry, butchering chickens, and painting signs. But, now he felt different, perhaps bigger than them all.

Fuhua didn't know much about Deming, he just heard that he is the Seven Standards Kung-Fu School's top fighter and has a reputation of defeating his opponents by stealing their desire to fight. Fuhua wasn't sure what this meant, maybe Deming knew how to outlast his opponents.

Fuhua walked for almost an hour when he noticed Deming sitting at a rundown outdoor tea house with a couple other men. Immediately Fuhua approached the table and made his declaration, "Deming, I'm Fuhua from the Purple Dragon Kung-Fu School, and I challenge you to a fight!"

Deming turned his head toward Fuhua and without even looking surprised said, "I have heard of you." Deming then cracked a smile, "You are here to challenge me to a fight," he paused taking a sip of tea, "then challenge away!"

"Yes," Fuhua said as he puffed up. "My kung-fu is better than your kung-fu!"

"Ah, is it?" Deming acted as if he was pondering the possibility and continued, "So if you are so certain that your kung-fu is better than mine, then why do you need to fight me? Are you trying to gain a reputation by defeating me? Are you truly interested in testing your skill? And if you win, does it mean that your school's kung-fu is better than my school's, or would it just mean that your personal skill is better than mine? Who sent you here? I bet no one. Are you really this predictable? Is the best fighter from the Purple Dragon School ready to take on the world?"

"Stop talking and fight me!" Fahue interrupted.

Deming kept talking, "Have you thought about the consequences of losing? Is reputation more important to you than true character?"

"Dammit, why won't you stand up and fight me?"

"Oh, sir Fuhua, I am fighting you. Can't you see?" Deming said with a stern face and continued, "Do you see questions as attacks—reasoning as techniques?"

Fuhua, frustrated to the breaking point, charged at Deming, "You're going to fight me now!" Fuhua then attempted to kick Deming out of his chair, but Deming simply moved so that the chair spun on one leg out of the way of Fuhua's kick.

"You attacked me and you haven't even brought a proper death waver for us to sign—and you attack a man while he sits in a chair."

"Fight me!" Fuhua yelled.

"As I said, I have been fighting you, you can't even see that you have missed the real challenge, and you are already defeated," Deming scolded.

Fuhua, stopped for a moment, lowered his hands from the ready position, then looked at Deming and bowed. "Someday I shall return and offer a proper challenge."

Fuhua turned and walked away, and on the tour back to his school, he considered all the things he still had to learn.

Real Battles

There are real battles in life that are not always physical.
Some don't put up much of a fight.
Give up on their family.
Don't see their kids.
Lose sight of their dreams.
Play dangerous games of addiction and mental slumming.
Kung-fu, or any martial arts training in general, is not all about fighting techniques or being a good fighter, it is about the fight for: love, family, vocation, health, and contributing to society.
Losing fights in the "ring" ultimately don't matter if you never realize the lessons of the ring; hard work and preparation, a sense of purpose, meeting a challenge, and the will to survive and to never give up.
Life does to us what our decisions allow.

Muse

Unstable is the muse
We try to capture it, give it therapy
Explode it
The muse wants to fight, to have adventure,
but is most at home in calm moments of reflection
It truly does want to be
transformed and preserved by art
As if reliving life is still living life
Smack the Muse
Pass it around

"Art reaches its greatest when devoid of self-consciousness. Freedom discovers man the moment he losses concern over what impression he is making or is about to make."
-- Bruce Lee

Darin Waugh

I am available to teach martial arts seminars and for speaking engagements. Please feel free to contact me at JKDMan@aol.com, and let's see what we can smack around!

WWW.Kiazen Publications.Com

www.ingramcontent.com/pod-product-compliance
Lightning Source LLC
Chambersburg PA
CBHW021241280526
45784CB00005B/2193